The Definitive Guide to PSM I

Passing the Professional Scrum Master™ I
exam on your first try.

Moritz Knueppel

Training, Consulting, Coaching
lead-in-agile.com
team@lead-in-agile.com

Self-published in July 2022
Fourth edition
Moritz Knueppel
Hermannstal 89
22119 Hamburg, DE
scrumguide@moritz-knueppel.eu

Table of Contents

Preface

Scrum offers a way of working that is breaking with seemingly conventional wisdom. Where there used to be strict hierarchies, we are discovering ways for teams to manage their work on their own. Where product development was divided into departments such as planning, requirements engineering, implementation, testing, documentation and release, we are discovering ways to build small teams that are capable of all of this. And perhaps most importantly of all, where projects used to take years, we are now discovering ways to deliver value within a month and often even more quickly than that.

What is this book for?
This book will grant you an overview of the Scrum framework, provide context for many of its ideas and rules and provide you all the knowledge necessary to pass Scrum.org's PSM I exam. This book sticks to the current Scrum Guide and marks additional practices explicitly, allowing you to understand what is (Core) Scrum and what are helpful things to use along-side Scrum.

How is this book structured?
Scrum.org advocates for the idea of Test-Driven-Development (TDD) in software development. This means we first define the tests that our new product increment must fulfill and then work our way there. Analogously, this book will start each section with questions that prepare you for PSM I.
The book will begin by introducing why agile development, of which Scrum is the most well-known and popular approach, is on the rise. It will then explain Scrum's roles, its events and its artifacts.

Finally, you will receive detailed information on the Professional Scrum examinations to prepare for PSM I.

What sets this book apart?
There are a number of books on the market that aim to prepare you for PSM I, some good, some rather questionable.
If you buy a car, you wish to buy it from a reputable brand at a reputable vendor to be sure of its quality and performance. Equally, you'd want to learn Scrum from a highly knowledgeable source. Regarding Scrum.org's exams, I can say with absolute certainty that there is no PSM I preparation book by an author more familiar with the Scrum.org exams. Why? Because I have taken and passed literally every Scrum.org exam there is.

MORITZ KNÜPPEL
mknueppel94@gmail.com

Moritz's Certifications

Beyond this book
If, after reading this book, you are interested in learning more about Agile Leadership, Scrum, and Kanban, visit my website and book a training course (German or English) for your organization under https://lead-in-agile.com

Why pursue a Professional Scrum certification

- Professional Scrum certifications are recognized as at least among the two most valuable basic-level Scrum certifications, alongside the Scrum Alliance's Certified Scrum certifications. Due to its high passing requirements, the Professional Scrum ones are often considered the more valuable one among the two.

- The Professional Scrum certifications are awarded by Scrum.org, which was founded and to this day is still supported by Ken Schwaber, one of the co-founders of Scrum and maintainers of the Scrum Guide.

- Professional Scrum has the highest quality standard among the various Scrum certifications in the market. Rather than just handing you the certification after attending a class, you have to take an exam, which has a difficult passing grade of 85%!

- Professional Scrum certifications do not require you to take a class. While attending an official Scrum.org class can be a rewarding experience, especially on the more advanced levels, you are not obligated to do so. Preparing on your own and passing the exam is sufficient.

- Once you receive your Professional Scrum certification, it will not expire and does not require the payment of renewal fees.

Preparations for PSM I

Basic information
- Duration: 60 minutes
- Question: 80; multiple-choice, multi-select, true/false
- Passing score: 85%

Taking the PSM I feels like a big step, primarily due to the uncertainty of what to expect. The average time that can be spent per question is 45 seconds, leading to a fast-paced exam that leads many to believe it will be stressful. The relatively high passing grade of 85% means that out of the 80 questions, only 12 may be answered incorrectly.

After having taken and passed all of Scrum.org's exams and having guided numerous people through their preparation process for PSM I and the similar PSPO I, I gained an understanding of how the exams are built and how to prepare for them efficiently and effectively.

All the knowledge necessary to pass the PSM I exam is contained in this book. While this book is much more compact than others you may find in the market, it contains the distilled essence of what you will need to pass the exam, without lengthy texts about non-essential aspects.

To prepare properly for the exam, read the entire book carefully at least once, ideally twice. Try each time to answer the questions at the beginning of each chapter prior to reading it.

Once you have finished your reading, take advantage of Scrum.org's Scrum Open Assessment. Each attempt contains 30 questions from the same pool as the PSM I questions.

If you attempt the Scrum Open multiple times, you are very likely to find some of the same questions during your actual exam. Knowing the answer to those questions will save you important time that you can use on other questions. Therefore, take this preparation exam multiple times.

A good benchmark for when you are ready is:

- You pass the Scrum Open three times in a row,
- With 100% each time,
- In under 10 minutes each (giving you 20 seconds per question on average).

For further example questions, you can use the PSM I mock exam on my website https://Scrum-Exams.info

Complexity, Empiricism, Scrum

Question	True	False
In a waterfall approach, feedback is usually acquired early and continuously throughout the process.		
Complexity can be addressed well through extensive up-front planning.		
Empiricism is based on the notion that we can determine everything rationally before taking action.		
Scrum is based on empiricism.		
Scrum is based on lean thinking.		
Scrum prescribes rules, roles, values, artifacts, and events.		
Scrum is a process.		
Scrum is a methodology.		
Scrum is a framework.		
Scrum uses an iterative approach.		
Scrum uses an incremental approach.		

--- Context: This part is included to provide context and is not part of the Scrum Guide ---

Traditional Product Development with Waterfall

When building a new product, we often see the following happen in the organization:

The initial idea is developed and product managers are assigned. These work out the ideas of the product, conduct market research, determine overarching requirements and set out a roadmap for the development.

Next up, tasks are handed over to project managers, who are in charge of the day-to-day business of managing the project of building the product. Under their supervision, more detailed requirements are gathered, typically by individuals with titles such as Requirement Engineer.

Once all the requirements have been gathered, Solution Architects develop a plan for technical implementation, including things like architecture and tech-stack to be used. Based on these plans, they also determine how long the development will need and what budget is necessary.

This plan is then executed by developers, who turn the requirements into the product as defined by the plan developed by the Solution Architects.

Lastly, the final product is tested by Quality Assurance people, who verify that the product suffices the quality standards. It is then released to the users for the first time since the development process began.

Once the product is live, it is handed over to another team, responsible for its operation and maintenance.

This process is called waterfall development, as information flows from one stage to the next.

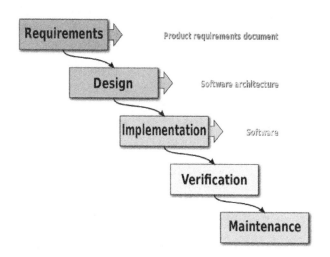

Risks with Waterfall Development

Approaches like the waterfall development assume that every part of the chain works as expected, that every plan made can be executed as planned and that no changes arise. This may work well for simple problems, but for complex problems, this is rarely the case. In each step, assumptions are made that may or may not be correct. The larger and thus often more complex a product is, the more the risks of these assumptions compound and the more likely it is that the development effort will fail.

Complexity

When we speak of complexity, we mean a specific definition. A problem is complex if the relationship between action and reaction cannot be known in advance. Take, for example, the development of a mobile app. The development has finished, testing is done, the app works reliably. Whether or not the market will react positively to it, whether people will be willing to download and even pay for it, is not known. While we can take steps such as market research beforehand, there is no guarantee that releasing our app (action) will lead to a successful acceptance in the marketplace (desired reaction).

In product development, many aspects are complex: market reactions, the interactions within a team, technical problems arising throughout the development effort, and so on. In none of these cases can a definitive statement be made beforehand. Even extensive planning cannot reasonably address complex problems.

Some problems are not only complex but also adaptive. This means that the relationship between action and reaction changes over time. A software that is released and considered user-friendly in 1999 will hardly satisfy any user 20 years later. The definition of user-friendliness has changed over time. Releasing the software (action) may have led to happy customers (reaction, old) in the last millennium, but is looked upon skeptically at best today (reaction, new).

So how does Scrum help us address complex and even complex adaptive problems?

--- End Context ---

Empiricism

Scrum's theoretical foundations lie in the idea that our knowledge comes not from long-term planning but from experience. Rather than make long-reaching assumptions, we should make our decisions based on what we have known from experience.

Therefore, to make decisions, we need to try things, learn from the outcomes, and adjust our plans. Considering that we are dealing not only with complex but complex adaptive problems, we take nothing for granted. Even the knowledge we gained through experiments can become obsolete, so we need to run these experiments regularly.

Empiricism requires three factors:
- Transparency – we need to be able to see and understand the things that are relevant.
- Inspection – we need to frequently take a look at the things that affect our work.
- Adaptation – we need to make adjustments if through inspection we gain the insight that another or new approach may be more successful.

Scrum and Empiricism

Scrum is a framework built upon the idea of empiricism. It prescribes rules, roles, values, events and artifacts, all of which are designed to maximize opportunities for empiricism. Every aspect in Scrum aims towards fostering transparency, allowing for frequent inspection and empowering adaptation.

It is important to note that while Scrum comes with prescriptions in the form of mandatory rules, roles, values, events and artifacts, it is a framework. Within Scrum, teams are free to choose whatever approach they think is appropriate. How the development takes place is left to the teams. This follows the idea that those closest to an issue generally know the most about it and are best at making the right decision. Thus, Scrum is neither a process nor a methodology but a framework. It provides a container within which teams can self-manage their work, including the application of processes and methodologies, as long as they do not violate the ideas of Scrum.

For people unfamiliar with Scrum, the most characteristic thing when learning about it usually is that it develops products in Sprints. We will go into detail about Sprints later; at this point, it is only necessary to understand that to address complex adaptive problems, Scrum takes an iterative, incremental approach.

Incremental means that the entire product is not built completely and then shown to the users, but rather smaller, functioning versions are built successively, allowing the team to gather feedback and make adjustments if necessary.

Iterative means that Scrum Teams work in cycles or iterations, called Sprints, in which planning, development, gathering feedback and process improvements are conducted. A Sprint lasts at most one month and is often even shorter than that.

This combination ensures that learning is incorporated regularly, and even changing conditions are quickly detected and the team can react to them.

Furthermore, Scrum is light-weight. The entire Scrum Guide only spans 13 pages to define the entirety of Scrum. That is because Scrum prescribes only the essentials and leaves a lot of freedom to those applying the framework. This reflects Scrum's foundation in lean thinking.

Answers to the questions in order:
False; False; False; True; True; True; False; False; True; True; True

Scrum Team

Question	True	False
The roles on the Scrum Team are Product Owner, Developer and Scrum Master.		
Project Manager (PM) is a possible role within a Scrum Team		
Scrum Teams are cross-functional.		
The self-managing of a Scrum Team is unlimited.		

The Scrum Team, as a small, highly flexible and adaptive team, is described as the essence of Scrum. Scrum Teams are usually 10 people or fewer in size to ensure that those who are part of it can communicate with each other effectively and can make necessary changes quickly. This makes Scrum Teams more agile than more conventional corporate structures, where work is split between different departments, each with its own management structure, to which it is difficult to make changes.

The work in the Scrum Team is divided into so-called "accountabilities". Formerly, there were referred to as "roles", and throughout this book this technically now out-dated terminology will be used for the sake of readability.
Scrum recognizes only the following three roles in a Scrum Team:

- The Product Owner, a single person who manages the Product Backlog and determines the direction of the product development through the Product Goal; this role may be filled as a part-time role by a Developer or Scrum Master, though especially the latter may not be advisable.

- The Scrum Master, a single person who supports the Product Owner, Developers and organization in delivering high-value products by spreading Scrum; this role may be filled as a part-time role by a Developer or Product Owner, though especially the latter may not be advisable.
- The Developers, a group of people responsible for the development work, i.e., turning Product Backlog items (e.g., in the format of User Stories) into a working piece of product.

All of these roles must be filled in a Scrum Team. There are no other roles in a Scrum Team!

A Scrum Team is characterized by three crucial aspects: cross-functionality, self-management, and shared ownership.

Cross-functionality describes the ability of the Scrum Team to deliver a Done product increment without the need for external help, e.g., by database specialists or a QA department. All skills required must be present within the team.

Self-management is the ability and empowerment of the Scrum Team to determine what to work on and how to do it. The Product Owner determines what Product Backlog items the team will work on, the Developers decide how they turn Product Backlog items into an increment.

To be effective in its coordination and internal communication, the team should not be too large. When there are too many people, the complexity of organizing and conducting meetings and keeping everybody synchronized becomes impractical. Therefore, the whole Scrum Team should typically consist of 10 members or fewer, including Developers, Product Owner and Scrum Master.

While not an explicit rule in the Scrum Guide, it is good practice to have teams be long-lived, meaning that the team's composition does not change frequently if not needed. If a long-term need is identified, the staffing of the team may be changed. However, a short-term realization that a Sprint cannot be finished would not justify adding a (temporary) new member to the team. Any change will temporarily reduce productivity, as a new person needs to be worked into their position and the team dynamics need to adjust.

Shared ownership describes the idea that the Scrum Team as a whole is responsible for the outcome. While in waterfall, there may be sub-teams (e.g., "programmers" and "testers"), Scrum recognizes no titles and no sub-teams within the group of Developers. Everybody is collectively accountable for the outcome of the whole team. While a person may still specialize primarily in testing, all of the Developers are responsible for testing to be conducted and have to figure out a way collectively to ensure it takes place. It is important to note that this also applies to (the lack of) internal hierarchies: Scrum Teams do not have concepts like tech leads, team leads, or an explicit internal junior-senior-hierarchy; all members are equally responsible for the outcome and equally responsible for working towards common goals.
Furthermore, the Product Owner, Scrum Master and the Developers share the responsibility that the Scrum Team as a whole produces a valuable product increment.

It's important to note that self-management is not completely unlimited, but takes place within the limits set by the organization within which the development takes place. While a Product Owner decides on the priorities for development and the Developers decide how to best implement the requirements, the Scrum Team does not usually get to decide on aspects like how many hours everybody works, their own salaries or broader corporate strategies that have direct effects on the team's work.

Answers to the questions in order:
True; False; True; False

Product Owner

Question	True	False
The Product Owner role is that of a value maximizer.		
The Product Backlog changes over time.		
The Product Goal provides an overarching direction for the Product Backlog.		
The Product Owner can delegate accountability for the Product Backlog.		
The Product Owner protects the Developers from external work requests.		
A Scrum Team can have multiple Product Owners.		
When multiple Scrum Teams work on a product, each team has its own Product Backlog.		

The Product Owner is often described as a value maximizer or value optimizer. They are responsible for determining the direction in which the product development effort is heading. For this, the Product Owner is responsible for engaging with the stakeholders to gather feedback to better understand the needs the product should meet. The Product Owner also maximizes the value of the product and of the work delivered by the Developers by supporting their understanding of the product, the stakeholder needs and the Product Backlog items in a Sprint.

Unlike Product Managers or Project Managers, neither of which exist on a Scrum Team, the Product Owner is not in charge of the Developers. The Product Owner is concerned with *what* the

Developers work on and to ensure they understand *why. How* the Developers do their work is up to the Developers.

The Product Owner manages the Product Backlog and is the only one accountable for it. The Product Backlog is a list of items, that reflects what is currently known about the product and the requirements that should be implemented. Unlike a project plan in waterfall, the Product Backlog is not static. It evolves as more is learned, e.g., through feedback from stakeholders, and is constantly updated and reordered. The order of the Product Backlog reflects what the Product Owner believes to be the most valuable next steps.

The Product Backlog ordering reflects what is called the Product Goal. The Product Goal is the desired future state of the product, whereas the Product Backlog describes the way to achieve that goal. The Product Goal is an overarching goal for the Scrum Team to ensure focus and alignment. This goal may change over time, if the previous goal has been achieved or is abandoned if it is no longer relevant.

The Product Owner may delegate some of the work of managing the Product Backlog to others, but they cannot pass the accountability to others!

All work the Developers do originates from the Product Backlog. This allows the Product Owner effective control of the direction in which the development is going. It also brings with it the responsibility to protect the Developers from interruptions. When somebody requests the Developers to work on something not in the Product Backlog, they should turn down that request and send that person to talk to the Product Owner.

It is important to understand that the Product Owner is the final decision maker regarding the direction of the product. In this capacity, their decision must be respected, both by the Developers and the management. This also necessitates that there is only one Product Owner per Scrum Team. Only this way can it be ensured that there is one person to make the final decisions. One product has one Product Backlog, for which one Product Owner is accountable, regardless of how many Scrum Teams work on the same product.

Answers to the questions in order:
True; True; True; False; True; False; False

Developers

Question	True	False
The Developers are responsible for turning Product Backlog items into an increment of working product.		
It is okay for Developers to work with an external specialist on a regular basis to develop an increment.		
The Product Owner is responsible for providing estimates of Product Backlog items.		
The Scrum Team owns the Sprint Backlog		
Managers and the Product Owner may use the Daily Scrum to inquire about the progress.		
A Scrum Team can add or remove Developers without any drops in productivity.		
There can be a person with the title of "tester" among the Developers.		

Developers in Scrum are responsible for turning requirements from the Product Backlog into a working product increment. All the work necessary for this is done within the team. Waterfall divides the development into phases such as design, coding, and testing and often assigns a different team to each step. In Scrum, things such as design, coding, and testing are typical parts of the development work, which is performed by the Developers, in software development.

The Developers are given their own artifact, their own event in Scrum and the right to estimate the size of Product Backlog items:

- The Sprint Backlog is the list of items the Developers believe they can implement in the Sprint and a plan on how to achieve this. The Sprint Backlog is owned exclusively by the Developers; nobody else has control over it or can change it without the Developers' consent.
- The Daily Scrum is an event exclusively for the Developers. In it, the Developers inspect the progress and plan the next steps. Nobody can tell the Developers how to run it, and nobody else has a right to participate as a non-Developer. This event is not a status meeting in which the Product Owner or management can get updated about the progress; it is an internal meeting of, for and by the Developers.
- The Developers provide the estimates for how much effort they believe they will need to implement a specific item from the Product Backlog and estimates of how much they believe they can deliver in a Sprint.

Answers to the questions in order:
True; False; False; False; False; False; False

Scrum Master

Question	True	False
The Scrum Master is a conventional leadership position.		
The Scrum Master provides guidance; they teach and coach.		
The Scrum Master supports the Developers by removing impediments.		
The Scrum Master should solve all of the Scrum Team's problems.		
The Scrum Master position is a management position.		

Within the Scrum framework, the Scrum Master often leads their team from the stance of a servant-leader to their team and their organization. This means that unlike more conventional leadership styles, they derive their impact not from being in charge of others and ordering them to do things but by enabling and empowering others. Among other things, this usually takes the following forms:

- Teaching Scrum within the Scrum Team, to the organization, and to relevant stakeholders
- Coaching the Product Owner about Product Backlog management, the Scrum Team about good practices of Scrum, and the management of the organization how best to interact with and support the Scrum Team
- Removing impediments, making sure the Scrum Team has nothing in the way of successful development work
- Facilitating some or all of the Scrum Events, as needed or requested

It is important to note that within the context of the Scrum Team, the Scrum Master rarely makes any decisions. Rather, they provide advice and support and guide people towards reaching the best possible decision.

Furthermore, it is important to note that the Scrum Master must try to coach the Developers towards self-management, letting them remove as many issues they face on their own and only helping when success is not possible otherwise. The term "impediment" in the context of the Scrum Master is to be understood as issues that go beyond the self-management of the Developers. Internal conflicts of the Developers should be resolved by the team; structural issues such as management expecting regular reports are an impediment a Scrum Master should deal with.

The Scrum Master is responsible for ensuring that Scrum is properly understood by the Scrum Team and by those relevant to the process. Therefore, the Scrum Master is sometimes called the "manager of the Scrum process". While they are not responsible for managing people, they are responsible for planning how to improve the Scrum awareness and to determine and implement necessary steps to achieve this goal, i.e., for managing Scrum.

Most crucial among the things that a Scrum Master must ensure are understood are:
• Product Backlog management - by the Product Owner
• Empirical product management - especially by the Product Owner
• How to effectively support a Scrum Team - by the management

- The purpose of the Scrum Events - by the Scrum Team
- The durations of timeboxes and their purpose - by the Scrum Team

Answers to the questions in order:
False; True; True; False; True

Scrum Events

Question	True	False
There are six different Scrum Events.		
All Scrum Events except for the Sprint happen during a Sprint.		
Timeboxed means an event must take at least a certain amount of time.		
All Scrum Events are timeboxed.		
Participation in Scrum Events is optional.		
Product Backlog refinement is one of the Scrum Events.		

In order to ensure that empiricism can take place, Scrum prescribes a number of mandatory events. Collectively, these events - if executed properly - are sufficient to ensure inspection and adaptation of all crucial aspects of the product development.

The Scrum Events are as follows:
• Sprint
• Sprint Planning
• Daily Scrum(s)
• Sprint Review
• Sprint Retrospective

The Sprint acts as a container; all other events take place within a Sprint. To ensure that the team works efficiently and in a focused manner, all events have maximum durations defined by the Scrum Guide. This is called timeboxing. Furthermore, participation in the Scrum Events is mandatory (if possible), as this is the only way to ensure the necessary transparency to allow for inspection and adaptation.

Many teams have regular Product Backlog refinement meetings within their Sprints, sometimes wrongly called the "sixth Scrum Event". While the activity of Product Backlog refinement is encouraged by the Scrum Guide, it is not a formal Scrum Event, as it does not have to take place in the form of a meeting, nor every Sprint.

Answers to the questions in order:
False; True; False; True; False; False

The Sprint

Question	True	False
Sprints make Scrum iterative.		
The timebox of a Sprint is one calendar month maximum.		
Working in Sprints, especially in short ones, limits risk by limiting the time and effort that are potentially wasted.		
The Sprint length may change frequently.		
There can be a time in-between Sprints.		
The output of a Sprint is a potentially releasable Increment.		
The Sprint supports Scrum's incremental approach.		
The Developers may choose to cancel a Sprint.		

As we established earlier, in product development, we are dealing with complex adaptive problems, meaning with problems that we can only learn about through experimentation and which can change over time. Therefore, we need to inspect and adapt repeatedly. This is the foundation for the iterative and incremental approach Scrum employs.

Planning to develop something, developing it while regularly inspecting the progress, inspecting whether or not the result is valuable and finding possible improvements to the process; all this is repeated regularly. Each of these activities manifests in a Scrum Event, all of which are contained in a Sprint. Scrum is iterative because these activities happen over and over again in Sprints.

A Sprint may be up to one calendar month in length, i.e., its timebox is one month. A Scrum Team may also choose their Sprints to be shorter. A Sprint should be long enough to produce something useful but as short as possible to limit the risk of producing something that turns out to not be valuable. This could be the case through changes in the market, uncertainty regarding stakeholder requirements, or the technology used. Short Sprints limit risk by limiting the time and effort that are potentially wasted if the result of a Sprint needs to be completely thrown away.

The Sprint length should remain constant over time.

A Sprint begins with the Sprint Planning, after which the Developers start their work. Every day, the Developers conduct a Daily Scrum. The Sprint ends with the Sprint Review and the Sprint Retrospective. Immediately after a Sprint ends, the next Sprint begins.

The output of a Sprint is an Increment, meaning the product before the Sprint (if there was one) plus at least one added useful outcome, e.g., a piece of new functionality. Rather than building the entire product in one go and having a useful version at the end of the development, potentially years later, in Scrum every Sprint produces all least one Increment that could be released into the market. This is why Scrum is described as following an incremental approach, supported by the use of Sprints.

A Sprint takes as long as its defined timebox. It may not exceed this duration. The only reason a Sprint may end before its timebox expires is if the Product Owner determines that the goal that the Sprint was supposed to achieve is no longer feasible or worth pursuing. This is called "cancelling a Sprint". Stakeholders, the Scrum Master, and the Developers may encourage this step to be taken; the decision is exclusively up to the Product Owner, however.

Answers to the questions in order:
True; True; True; False; False; True; True; False

Sprint Planning

Question	True	False
The Scrum Master forecasts the Developers' capacity empirically, based on past Sprints' performance.		
The whole Scrum Team participates in the Sprint Planning.		
The Sprint Goal is created by the Product Owner.		
The plan in the Sprint Backlog must include all the work for all the items.		
During the Sprint Planning, items are assigned to individual Developers.		
The Developers may remove items from the Sprint Backlog during the Sprint without any approval from the Product Owner.		
The Developers owns the Sprint Backlog collectively; no member is responsible for any single part of it.		
For a four-week Sprint, the timebox of the Sprint Planning is eight hours.		

The Sprint Planning serves to clarify three questions:
- Why is the Sprint valuable?
- What is the product at the end of the Sprint supposed to deliver that it cannot do now?
- How will this be achieved?

In the beginning of the Sprint Planning, the Product Owner proposes how the product could gain in value through the work that can be done in the Sprint.

Developers and Product Owner discuss much they believe to be able to deliver. The Developers provide a forecast of what they believe they can achieve. The metric is left up to the Scrum Team: this is often a numerical value in Story Points, which is referred to as velocity, though this is an optional practice not prescribed by the Scrum Guide. Once it is clear how much the Developers will be able to achieve, the Product Owner discusses the objective this Sprint is supposed to achieve and which items from the Product Backlog would serve this purpose.

The entire Scrum Team together crafts a Sprint Goal, an overarching goal which the work of the Developers is supposed to achieve through the delivery of an Increment. This Sprint Goal serves as the purpose of the Sprint; all plans may and should be adjusted to ensure this goal is met.

The Developers pull as many items from the Product Backlog as they believes they can achieve into their own backlog for the Sprint, which is called the Sprint Backlog. Once this is done, the Developers develop a plan on how to implement the selected items. In this process, there may be a back-and-forth with the Product Owner, as multiple possible solutions are evaluated and discussed.

The plan may include all selected items being planned through; however, it must at least plan the work for the coming few days. Planning too far ahead may result in waste, as new learnings throughout the Sprint may alter the basis upon which the plans were built.

The created plan then becomes part of the Sprint Backlog. This plan addresses how items will be implemented, not who will implement them. As the

Developers are collectively responsible for producing an Increment, nobody is assigned individual items, neither during the Sprint Planning nor throughout the Sprint.

The Sprint Planning is timeboxed to 8 hours. For Sprints shorter than one month, it is usually shorter; however, the timebox always remains 8 hours. The outputs of the event are the Sprint Goal and the Sprint Backlog. The Scrum Team commits to achieving the Sprint Goal, not the items in the Sprint Backlog. This allows for flexibility: if, for example, individual items turn out to take more time than expected (which is very possible in a complex environment), other items may be removed from the Sprint Backlog to compensate. This, however, requires agreement from the Product Owner.

Throughout the Sprint, the Sprint Backlog is likely to change as more is learned, and development work progresses. The Sprint Backlog is owned exclusively by the Developers, who are the only ones allowed to update it but also the only ones responsible for doing so.

Answers to the questions in order:
False; True; False; False; False; False; True; True

Daily Scrum

Question	True	False
The timebox of the Daily Scrum depends on the number of Developers participating.		
The Daily Scrum is held in the same place and at the same time every (work) day.		
The Developers inspect the Product Backlog during the Daily Scrum.		
The Daily Scrum is a key opportunity to raise impediments.		
Burn-down charts are one way to visualize progress and remaining work.		
The Daily Scrum is a good opportunity for managers to inquire about the team's progress.		
The Product Owner actively participates in the Daily Scrum.		
The Scrum Master teaches or coaches the Developers to keep the Daily Scrum within its timebox.		

The key outputs from the Sprint Planning are the Sprint Goal and the Sprint Backlog. Throughout the Sprint, the Developers work towards achieving the Sprint Goal by following the plan laid out in the Sprint Backlog. As product development is a complex problem, this plan will likely need to change as more is learned throughout the Sprint. Thus, the Developers inspect and adapt the Sprint Backlog every day during the Daily Scrum.

The Daily Scrum is a meeting of the Developers and timeboxed to 15 minutes, regardless of Sprint length or number of members of the Developers. To reduce complexity, it takes place every (work) day in the same place and at the same time. The Developers use the Daily Scrum to create transparency over the current status of the development and to plan the next steps towards achieving the Sprint Goal. The goal of the Daily Scrum is to make the achievement of the Sprint Goal more likely.

During the Daily Scrum, the Developers may raise impediments, which may be passed along to the Scrum Master to address.

A common format for the Daily Scrum is known as "the three questions". Until the 2013 Scrum Guide it was the prescribed format, with the 2017 Scrum Guide it was made optional and the 2020 Scrum Guide does not mention it at all. This possible format asks every member to share:
• What have they done yesterday towards achieving the Sprint Goal?
• What will they do today towards achieving the Sprint Goal?
• Were any impediments encountered while working towards the Sprint Goal?

While not prescribed by the Scrum Guide, the Daily Scrum may be supported by visualisations of internal metrics such as a Sprint Burndown Chart, which plots the remaining work in the Sprint (often measured in Story Points) against a trend line aiming towards zero work left at the end of the Sprint.

It is important to note that the purpose of the Daily Scrum is internal synchronization and inspection and adaptation of the Sprint Backlog:

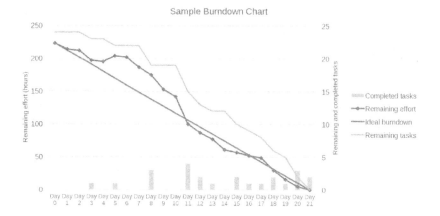

Sample Burndown Chart

- Completed tasks
- Remaining effort
- Ideal burndown
- Remaining tasks

The meeting is not supposed to be a status update for the members of the management, the Scrum Master or the Product Owner. As an internal meeting of the Developers, only the Developers participate, while the Scrum Master may facilitate the event if requested or necessary, and the Product Owner may listen to the meeting without actively participating. They may only actively participate if they are also part-time Developers and then take part in their function as Developers.

The Scrum Master's only responsibility toward the Developers regarding the Daily Scrum is to teach and/or coach them to keep the meeting within its 15 minute timebox.

Neither is the meeting supposed to contain in-depth technical discussions. These often take place immediately after the Daily Scrum.

Possible outputs of the Daily Scrum are a revised plan in the Sprint Backlog and/or the insight that not all items in the Sprint Backlog will likely be achieved in the Sprint. This insight is then shared with the Product Owner, and the Developers and Product

37

Owner work towards reducing the scope of the Sprint Backlog by removing lower priority items, while keeping the Sprint Goal achievable.

The act of daily inspection and adaptation of the Sprint Backlog leads to the Daily Scrum being referred to as a key inspect-and-adapt meeting. Lowering its frequency would lower the team's ability to inspect and adapt.

Answers to the questions in order:
False; True; False; True; True; False; False, True

Sprint Review

Question	True	False
The Increment is the sum of all the Done work during a Sprint.		
The Increment must be usable.		
If there are no organizational guidelines, the Scrum Team defines its own Definition of Done.		
Items that are not Done may be included in the Increment if the Product Owner approves.		
The Sprint Review involves the Scrum Team and key stakeholders.		
The Sprint Review is a formal status-meeting.		
For a two-week Sprint, the timebox of the Sprint Review is four hours.		

Throughout the Sprint, the Developers implement Product Backlog items from their Sprint Backlog to achieve the Sprint Goal. All the work of the Sprint is integrated into what is called the Increment. The Increment is one of the Scrum Artifacts and possesses the following three key attributes:

- The Increment is the sum of all the work that is Done, meaning complying with the Definition of Done (see below), integrated with the previous Sprint's increment.
- The Increment is delivered by the Developers as a result of its work toward the Sprint Goal.
- The Increment must be "usable", meaning that if the Product Owner chooses to release it, it must be

releasable without a large delay or effort and work for the user.

The Definition of Done is a tool for transparency. It defines the criteria, which every implemented Product Backlog item must fulfill to be included in the Increment. The Definition of Done is either provided by the standards of the organization in which the product is being developed, often referring to guidelines of an internal Quality Assurance department or defined by the Scrum Team, if no such standards exist. The Definition of Done covers both functional and non-functional requirements.

Before the Sprint Review, all the Done work is included in the Increment. Work that is not Done is not included but rather returns to the Product Backlog. It is then left to the Product Owner to decide how to proceed with it, e.g. include it in the next Sprint. This ensures that the entire Increment complies with the Definition of Done, allowing a transparent minimal quality standard, both towards the Scrum Team internally, as well as towards stakeholders, e.g., during the Sprint Review.

The Sprint Review is an event during which the Scrum Team meets with key stakeholders, who are invited by the Product Owner, to inspect the Increment. This meeting is intended to be informal and conducted as a workshop rather than a status-meeting; stakeholders, Product Owner and Developers inspect the Increment together, often by trying it out together. The goal of the meeting is to gather feedback from the stakeholders about the current state of the product. This feedback is incorporated by the Product Owner into the Product Backlog, which provides the next steps for the product development.

Other issues that may be addressed during the Sprint Review are projected release dates as well as discussions about timeline, budget, and marketplace changes. A common topic is whether or not the Increment should be released into the market. Releasing an Increment must always be possible but does not have to take place every Sprint. The decision to release is up to the Product Owner.

The event is timeboxed to four hours. For Sprints shorter than one month, it is usually shorter; however, the timebox always remains four hours.

Answers to the questions in order:
True; True; True; False; True; False; True

Sprint Retrospective

Question	True	False
The Sprint Retrospective is the last event to take place in a Sprint.		
The Definition of Done may be adjusted during the Sprint Retrospective.		
At least one high-priority item from the Sprint Retrospective is included in the Sprint Backlog of the next Sprint.		
The timebox of the Sprint Retrospective is three hours.		

The Sprint ends with the Sprint Retrospective. This event provides a formal opportunity for inspection and adaptation. The entire Scrum Team collaborates to inspect the current Sprint. All aspects are considered; most commonly cited in secondary literature are people, processes, and practices. Together, they try to identify possible improvements, aiming towards making the next Sprint more effective and more enjoyable.

The Scrum Master facilitates the Sprint Retrospective if needed or requested, otherwise, they participate as a fellow Scrum Team member. They are responsible, though, to encourage the rest of the team to continually improve.

A common subject of inspection and possible adaptation in the Sprint Retrospective is the Definition of Done. During the Sprint Retrospective, the Product Owner and the Developers have the chance to discuss the requirements necessary for the product to be of high quality. Over time, the quality is expected to increase; therefore, the Definition of Done may become more stringent over time.

To ensure that the outputs of the Sprint Retrospective are implemented, the Scrum Guide used to prescribe that at least one high-priority item from the Sprint Retrospective be included in the next Sprint Backlog. In the most recent update, this is no longer mandatory.

The event is timeboxed to three hours. For Sprints shorter than one month, it is usually shorter; however, the timebox always remains three hours.

Answers to the questions in order:
True; True; False; True

Scrum Values

The Scrum Guide defines a set of values. Living and embodying the values help a Scrum Team to conduct its work better, among other things, by creating greater transparency, allowing for better inspection and adaptation.

The five Scrum Values are:
• Commitment, to the goals of the Scrum Team
• Courage, to tackle difficult problems
• Focus, on the goals of the Scrum Team
• Openness, within the Scrum Team and between Scrum Team and stakeholders
• Respect, towards each other

Successfully living out these values will not only lead to a better Scrum application but also towards trust within the Scrum Team and between the Scrum Team and its stakeholders.

Common Misconceptions

Scrum offers a new way to approach problems that is very different from currently common ways. Thus, many people have misconceptions about Scrum, which are the result of applying conventional thinking to situations in the Scrum environment. In the following table, I will compare approaches from conventional project/product management with Scrum:

Topic	Conventional approach	Scrum
Sprint progress updates	Management updates the metrics about the progress of the developers' work throughout the development.	The Sprint Backlog is a tool of, for, and by the Developers. Updating the metrics is part of the self-management of the Developers.
Task Ownership	Individual items are often assigned to individual people, who are individually responsible for finishing.	The Developers are collectively responsible for the creation of the Increment during the Sprint and every item in the Sprint Backlog. No Developer owns any item individually.

Topic	Conventional approach	Scrum
Hardening phase	Phases of feature development may be followed by hardening phases, in which the undone work of the feature development is taken care of, e.g., non-functional requirements such as scalability.	Every Sprint delivers an increment that is Done. Thus, there is no hardening phase. "Hardening Sprints", as they are sometimes called, are not a valid construct in Scrum.
Crunch time	When a deadline needs to be met or a quota fulfilled, it often happens that developers are ordered to work overtime.	Scrum aims for sustainable development. When plans, which in Scrum are merely forecasts, cannot be met, they need to be adjusted, and this change must be made transparent.
Coordinate across teams	When multiple teams work together, the managers of these teams coordinate the collaboration.	When multiple teams work together, all members of all Developers are responsible for finding a proper way to collaborate.

Topic	Conventional approach	Scrum
Dev. launch	The first weeks of a project are often spent gathering all requirements, establishing a static plan and creating the architecture for the entire project.	The first Sprint is just like any other Sprint. Requirements are gathered as more is learned, plans change over time, and architecture emerges throughout the development. Thus, the first Sprint delivers a Done increment of at least one piece of new functionality. There is also no such thing as a "Sprint 0", taking place before the start of the development!
Role of management	Management supervises activities of those they are responsible for. This often includes measuring the work and directing individuals.	Scrum Teams are self-managing, they measure their own outputs and organize their work on their own. Management's role shifts towards supporting the Scrum Team and fostering more and better self-management.

Finally, the perhaps greatest misconception about Scrum is that it can be partially adopted. When a company starts to work in Sprints but, for example, does not have a Scrum Master or conducts no Sprint Retrospectives, this is not Scrum. It may still be better than their previous approach, but it is not Scrum.

Likewise, Scrum's vocabulary must be adopted. A company may claim to adopt Scrum but remains with the old non-Scrum terminology. Introducing Scrum is supposed to change things, to make existing problems transparent; refusing the terminology may make things easier for those involved, especially the management, but ultimately undermine the ability to detect change or for change to even happen.

Relevant terminology

There is a terminology surrounding Scrum, that is not explicitly in the Scrum Guide, but relevant to the PSM I certification. Those are:

Feature Team
A feature team is a Scrum Team that develops entire, usable features rather than individual parts of a feature. In an environment with only one Scrum Team, that team must be a feature team.

Layer Team
A layer team is a Scrum Team that develops parts of features in a specific layer, e.g., front-end, database, persistence layer, etc.
Multiple layer teams may work together with other Scrum Teams in developing one product. Every Sprint, their contributions must be integrated into functional, Done features.

Technical debt
This refers to the implied cost of additional rework caused by choosing an easy (limited) solution now, instead of using a better approach that would take longer. Technical debts lower transparency, as the Product Owner and stakeholders receive a wrong assumption about the current state of the product. Technical debt adding up will lead to development speed slowing down and the product potentially becoming unstable over time.

Story Points
A common format for Product Backlog items is that of the user story. In it, the requirement is typically provided in a format of "As an X, I want Y, so that I can Z". The Developers may estimate the effort

needed for a user story in a relative unit called story points.

Velocity
The velocity of a team typically refers to the number of story points delivered by the Developers during one Sprint.

Scrum.org Exams

As of July 2022, Scrum.org offers the following certifications:

- Professional Scrum Master (PSM I, II, III)
- Professional Scrum Product Owner (PSPO I, II, III)
- Professional Scrum Developer (PSD I)
- Professional Scrum with User Experience (PSU I)
- Professional Scrum with Kanban (PSK I)
- Scaled Professional Scrum (SPS)
- Professional Agile Leadership (PAL I)
- Professional Agile Leadership - EBM (PAL-EBM)

For most people, the first step into the certifications of Scrum.org is PSM I, which is by far the most rewarded certification, counting over 300,000 certified individuals worldwide. The currently rarest certifications are the most advanced ones: PSPO III and PSM III.

Lead in Agile provides trainings preparing for all levels of certification, including PSM III, to organizations in English and German. If you are interested, reach our via the contact form on the website: https://lead-in-agile.com

Scrum.org provides practice tests for its exams:

PSM I	Scrum Open
PSPO I	Product Owner Open
PSD I	Scrum Developer Open
PSK I	Scrum with Kanban Open
SPS	Nexus Open
PAL I	Agile Leadership Open
PAL-EBM	Evidence-Based Management Open

Image Sources

Disclaimer

Printed in Great Britain
by Amazon

42936213R00030